The Unspoken Cause of Auschwitz

Anthony Gifford

Other books by the author

Simeon's Gospel

Churches: A Time To Die – Hope For New Life

101 Things You Might Not Have Heard In Church

Dare To Share

Bread versus the Sword: The Fundamental Schism within Christianity and How It's Weaponization Threatens Our World

This is dedicated to Judy.

Table of Contents

Timeline

300 BC - Alexander conquers area

190 BC - Seleucids of Syria rule

166 BC - Jews revolt – Kingdom of Judah

63 BC – Pompey (Rome) takes Jerusalem

37 BC – Herod becomes king

4 BC – Herod dies, Judea partitioned

30 AD? – Jesus' death

40 – 65 Paul's ministry

70 – Fall of Jerusalem in Jewish War

71-100? – Writing of the Gospels

250 – First Jewish persecution by Christians

325 – Council of Nicaea

1070 – 1300 – Crusades

1520s – Martin Luther

1940s – Nazis death camps

Seeing that many others have undertaken to draw up the account of the events that have taken place among us…, I, in my turn, after carefully going over the whole story from the beginning, have decided to write an orderly account for you, Theophilus (Lover of God), so that you might learn, believe, and follow the teachings you have received. (Luke 1:1-4)

Preface

I write this in the full awareness that many Christians will find my treatment of the Gospels heretical and blasphemous. To them, the Bible is above questioning. All scriptures, especially the gospels, are the unquestioned, irrefutable, and perfect Word of God. They have been taught that the 'job' of the laity is to hear and believe the interpretation as given by those who are 'ordained' to do so. For them, questioning is a sign of disbelief, a lack of 'faith', perhaps, even a sign of the Devil.

I follow another and much older understanding, that of Jesus of Nazareth and other Jews. In this tradition, true questioning brings us closer to the Holy. We grow best, they have found, as we use our heads and hearts, with others, sharing our common doubts and possible answers, striving in this holy and imperfect world to make sense of the gifts and lives the Holy Creator has given us. In this ancient understanding, to *not* question, is to spiritually stagnate. This was the Way of Jesus of Nazareth. It's the Way I choose to live. So, I question and prod the Gospels, *not* because I want to weaken or destroy them, or the faith of others, but that I might get the most *out* of them. I value them enough to seek what they *first* meant. Only when I try my best to understand *that*, will I be most able to adopt and adapt that message to my own life and times.

The Question

My question is this: Why has one constant within Christianity been the impulse and license to persecute Jews? The very first corporate action of Christians when they had achieved influence and power, was to attempt to eradicate Judaism. In the late 300s AD, Augustine of Hippo saved many lives when he advised his fellow Christians to not kill *all* of them. He reasoned that since Jews had committed the *eternal* crime of killing the *eternal* Christ, they must suffer *eternally*. Hence, he reasoned, enough of them must be spared so they could propagate and thus, be killed *forever*. This was the 'Father of Christian Theology'.

From the middle 200's AD to now, the number of recorded violent acts against Jews, by Christians, is in the many hundreds; millions, obviously, if individuals are counted. Many more, of course, went unrecorded. To even list the main events of lootings, forced conversions, pogroms, mass killings and major expulsions, would take many pages. Jews have been expelled from eighty countries in Europe from 250 to 1948 AD. There was an average of one major 'event' every twenty-one years. We will not be trying to chronicle these terrible events, only mentioning those that are symbolic and will help us to see the larger picture.

Jews were banned from their homeland by the Romans after their second revolt in the second century AD. Denied citizenship in all Christian lands, they survived by their smarts, keeping in good communication among themselves. Being constantly vulnerable to the whims of local politics, they became well educated in 'mobile' trades and crafts, knowing that every few generations they might have to flee with what they could carry.

One notable and wonderful exception to this general picture needs to be shared. From the 500's to 900's a tribe known as Khazar ruled the area north of the Caucasus Mountains and lands north of the Caspian and Black Seas. This included the Crimea and what is now the Ukraine. When Islam erupted from the south in the 700's, the rulers of Khazar realized its precarious position, being squeezed between the two opposing religious powers, Islam and Christianity. To choose either religion was to invite war with the other. (Remember that the assumption was that every country was of one religion.) They chose a third alternative, Judaism, thus staving off invasions from both sides. It worked.

During the next several centuries, Jewry from even far away could go there for sanctuary. Many people in this area converted to Judaism and the faith thrived, being the first homeland for Jews since the year 70. Even in 1346 a Russian chronicle called the eastern Caucasus "The Land of the Jews". Today's Prime Minister of the Ukraine, Volodymyr Zelenskyy, is a Jew.

Ever wonder why so many Jews ended up in Eastern Europe? During the Crusades, Christians heading to the Holy Land often 'practiced' on Jews along the way, using the loot and sale of their properties to finance the war. To survive, Jews migrated north and east, out of the danger of the Crusaders' usual path.

A few hundred years later, the great reformer, Martin Luther, declared that Jews were not really human at all, worthy only to be slaves of slaves. France, under Napoleon Bonaparte, in the early 1800s, was the first European power to grant Jews citizenship.

Few countries were not complicit. All the world knew what Hitler was doing, yet the official stand of the Canadian government regarding Jews immigrating from Europe was "None is too many." (There's a great book by this same name.) When Hitler sent a boatload of Jews across the Atlantic in 1938, only two Latin American countries allowed some to land. We sent the rest back to the gas chambers. Until 1952 there were signs on public beaches in Toronto, Ontario, declaring *Dogs and Jews Not Allowed*.

Hardly a week goes by without a report of somewhere in the world where Jews are being threatened, harmed or killed. Last week, here in Kingston, there were anti-Semitic flyers put on cars. Kanye West is in the news today because of his public and unabashed anti-Semitism. His line of clothing has been dropped by many retailers, but much of the population will sympathize, and cry out about the lack of free speech allowed him. Just this month, (November 2022) the Ontario Government has stated that all grade six students should be taught about the Holocaust, recognizing that in the last year there had been at least fifty incidents of anti-Semitic hate crimes in Toronto alone. However, there will be no attention given to the source of the hatred that inspires these actions. The situation is common throughout the 'western' world.

What is the origin of this abiding hatred, this aberration that is the most deadly and persistent of the world's persecutions? Hardly a mere academic inquiry, this is literally a matter of life and death. To not seriously ask this question is to condemn and condone, regardless of our professed spirituality.

Ask any who hate the Jews. They'll easily and clearly tell you, whether or not they are churchgoers, *"It's in the Bible!"* Sadly, and tragically, they are correct. But even the *asking* of this simple question is not allowed. For all other crimes, the first question asked by investigating authorities is that of motive. There is one constant exception to this. In crimes against Jews, the question of motive is not asked. It is already known. It has been and is, part of Christianity. The fountain of hatred toward Jews is clearly in the New Testament. To the fundamentalist Christian, if you believe 'in the bible', you will hate the Christ-Killing Jews.

Tragically, no authority, legal, political or religious, will state this obvious fact. It is taboo. Its verbalization would be tantamount to questioning the Christian fundamental of the doctrine of *the inerrancy of scripture*. None dare to do so, even though a rather small percentage of our society still holds this dogma dear to their hearts.

The suspicion of Jews is now part of our collective tradition. Anti-Semitism has been engrained in us for 1700 years, whether or not we are traditional Christians.

In our culture, Jews are at risk. Why? The answer lies in the Gospels. Care/dare to look?

Let's take the Gospels seriously, seriously enough to try to view them as for the first time, neutrally, as if we haven't been 'taught' from/about them since our beginnings. Let's value them enough to ask the important questions we would ask of any ancient writing: Who wrote them? Why were they written and for whom? What were their assumed understandings, fears and traditions? What differences would these writings have made upon their lives? Only when we do our best to answer these questions of the past, can we faithfully begin to answer them for ourselves. To find the root of anti-Semitism, this *must* be our first task.

Background to the Gospels

The Land of the Jews, along with all the Eastern end of the Mediterranean, and most lands to the east, were conquered by Alexander the Great around 300 B.C. When he died soon after, the Greek Empire was divided into logical sub-kingdoms, each ruled by one of Alexander's primary generals. Judea was first ruled by the Ptolemies of Egypt. (Cleopatra was the last reigning member of that Greek family.) After a while, this changed, and the Syrian Greek Kingdom of the Seleucids ruled that land. The Seleucids became increasingly oppressive, for they correctly recognized the great differences between their cultural understandings and the those of the Jews. Example: Jews believed and acted as if the earth was holy, that all of creation was created 'Good', and understood that all people were God's children and should act accordingly. The Greeks believed that the 'spiritual' and 'physical' realms were completely separate. To them, the physical world (here) was not *good*, only necessary. Use it, abuse it. It didn't matter. Only the 'spiritual' counted.

Soon, even possessing a scroll of Jewish scripture was cause for death. The Greek-thinking rulers turned the Jerusalem Temple into a pig barn, the ultimate insult, and Judaism in all forms and customs, banned. In the 160's B.C. the Jews revolted under the Maccabaeus brothers and defeated the Seleucids, re-forming the 'Kingdom of God' in real terms. This Kingdom of Judea lasted for a century.

In 63 B.C. the Roman General Pompey marched into Jerusalem, claiming the area for Rome. They needed to control the land-route to Egypt. As an approved puppet of Rome, Herod (The Great) was soon appointed as the nominal ruler. The Jews were under no illusions, but, at least, there were no Roman soldiers in the streets and generally, things went OK.

When King Herod died in 4 B.C., the 'kingdom' was divided into four parts, two 'ruled' by the old Herod's sons, the other two by appointed governors. Roman soldiers were stationed throughout the land. No longer could Roman rule and occupation be denied. Paying tribute to another god was against the basis of Jewish understanding. ("Thou shalt have no other gods before me.") Since it stated right on the Roman coins that Caesar was a god, there was an immediate underground rebellion, the Zealot movement. The first revolt was only a year after the partition, when Judas of Galilee led the Zealots in revolt, raising the flag of the messiah, one anointed by Yahweh to rule as a godly king. Most Jews did not follow his flag and Judas and followers were easily defeated.

But the Zealot movement continued to grow. They assumed that at the right time, if the people were faithful (killing as many Romans and their supporters as possible), God would raise up from among them a messiah, who would lead the nation to independence and faithfulness. It had happened before when they had revolted against the Syrian Empire. Why not now? Into this cauldron of danger, intrigue, hopefulness and despair, Jesus began his movement.

The Jesus Movement

His message was simple: *God's Kingdom is Here. The choice is yours: Live in it or not.* The Kingdom was not just a belief, or something after death, but a Way of life, right now. It was one of communal sharing: to follow Jesus, people gave away what they didn't need and shared everything else in community. It was open to all: your background and past were of no concern. It was scandalously egalitarian: women were welcome, even apart from their husbands. It was confrontational in the classical prophetic tradition, embarrassing, offending and threatening to many, especially those of power and wealth, since it demanded justice and fairness for all. It reminded the people that it was against their very being, as Jews, to pay tribute to other gods. It was against all violence. (*Shalom* is a state of peace brought about through justice and love, not force.)

This combination set it apart from the other many Jewish understandings. It was in direct conflict with the *Herodians* (descendants of the old royalty, now working with the Romans), the *Sadducees* (the higher class of merchants and landowners, also happy with Roman rule), and the reclusive groups such as the *Essenes* that were leading 'pure' lives in remote desert areas.

Much of what Jesus said and did *was* encouraging to the *Zealots*, however, as they were desperately looking for a messiah to unite and lead them to victory. We know there were at least four Zealots within Jesus' group. Firstly, there is Judas Iscariot. *Iscariot* is a take-off for *sicarii*, a short dagger most favored by Zealot assassins. (Think *Mack-the-knife*.) We also have Simon the Zealot (Luke 6:15) and the two sons of Zebedee, called *Boanerges*, a colloquial reference to Zealots, meaning *Sons of Thunder*. (Mark 3:17)

The *Pharisees* were of the 'party' most similar to Jesus' teachings. As a group, their purpose was to interpret and apply the Jewish customs to be a joy to the people, not a burden. The gospels portray them as the 'bad guys', always arguing with Jesus, obviously being against him. In truth, history tells us the opposite. To be invited into a leading Pharisee's home for dinner and debate was as good-as-it-got. To debate scripture was a sign of social acceptance and honor. For Jews, now as then, debate is spiritual, educational and entertaining. No anger or opposition is implied.

Sadly, even Jesus' closest followers didn't understand the depth of his non-violent Calling and simply could not stop urging him to accept the mantel of the Zealot-driven *messiah*, someone to lead them in violent revolt against the hated Romans. Recall the times when Jesus' disciples were debating as to who among them would be sitting at Jesus' side when God's Kingdom had come? They were hardly thinking in esoteric or 'heavenly' terms. They were assuming that Jesus would actually conquer and rule as Messiah! None among them understood.

As the last resort, to help them understand, Jesus finally accepted the role, became Messiah-for-a-Day, enabling the Zealots to attain control of Jerusalem, even shutting down the Temple. Roman soldiers and Temple guards were outnumbered for that short time and did nothing but stay behind their walls. But, after the evening meal (Passover?), Jesus, instead of ordering the long-anticipated assault on the Romans and their allies, publicly rejected the role of a messiah. Abandoning those who were relying on his role in the violence, he left the safety of the city and returned to his vulnerable camp in the hills.

Pontius Pilate knew what was happening and quickly took advantage of the situation. A commando raid by Roman soldiers and/or Temple guards soon captured him and brought him back to the city. His formal trial was held the first thing the next morning. Under heavy Roman guards, he was executed as soon as possible, probably being tortured and injured to hasten his death.

The mandatory and prescribed three days of legal Roman proceedings were ignored, condensed into only a few hours. The spectacle of a public crucifixion that was designed to last easily a day or three, was speeded up to a minimum. Pontius Pilate was taking no chances of letting the Zealots re-organize. (This is the history that all people of that time knew and could not ignore, even two generations later, when the gospels were written.)

Two days later, while in hiding from the Romans, the followers who hadn't left the city, had life-changing experiences that could only be called a *Resurrection*. These affected them to such an extent that they found new life and hope, knowing they were to stay in Jerusalem until Jesus came again, from God's presence, this time, as the *cosmic* Messiah. They still refused to give up their messianic dream, still unable to understand the depth of Jesus' non-violent Kingdom.

As a community, they remained there for the next thirty years, becoming one more Jewish sect, respected, accepted and in competition with the others. Jesus' brother was known throughout the city as James the Just. Eventually they came to agree with the Zealots in believing that if they initiated a revolt against Rome, thus proving their faithfulness, God would deliver and save them with a messiah. Jesus' followers differed from the others only in that they already knew who the Messiah would be. They joined in the general revolt in 65 AD. Those original followers were wrong, again, and all perished, to the last, when, after four years of revolt and bloodshed, the Romans finally stormed Jerusalem in AD 70. All within the walls were killed. "No stone was left upon another."

Assuming the world would end and be reborn with the new Messiah, they hadn't tried to preserve anything from the past. The past didn't matter, for history would begin again, they knew, any day. Certain stories of Jesus and collections of his sayings were what they held of value. These had become timeless. But nothing else from the past mattered.

Paul (Greek name for Saul)

About ten years after Jesus' death, a sophisticated, well-educated and wealthy Jew from Tarsus changed everything. Saul of Tarsus, who obviously had been skeptical and against the upstart Jerusalem community, quite unexpectedly, experienced a vision of the Risen Jesus. From the event, Saul knew he was Called by God to share with Gentiles, the Good News that Adonai, the loving God of Creation, was now open to all people. Following the Way of Jesus was *The Way* for everyone to understand and do God's Will. All could follow the path of openness, justice, non-violence, egalitarianism, and lives of communal sharing, that Jesus had shown.

You could adopt and adapt this to your own culture, not worrying about Jewish customs. As all Jews knew, (the Jerusalem followers agreed), their laws (customs) were observed as signs and reminders of God's Call to Justice and Love. Obeying them did nothing in and of itself. Though helpful, they were not necessary to living faithfully to God's Will.

And where would Paul logically go to find 'approachable' Gentiles? Surprisingly to us, it was the Synagogues. Remember that all Gentile 'faiths' of that time were based on the understanding that the many dozens of gods were all powerful, but very capricious and untrustworthy. The concept of a Loving god was foreign to them. Gods of Love, in their traditions, were gods who could bestow romantic love upon humans, and did so, for a price. To them, religion was entirely based upon sacrifice. If you wanted a 'gift' that a certain god could provide, you went to that individual temple and paid what was required. A truly religious person paid all they could, just to keep the gods off their backs. The gods of the Gentiles did nothing for nothing.

There was little sense of community within most Gentile understandings. In their temples there were few large common spaces for gatherings. A petitioner went alone, or in small groups, made their sacrifices of money or items, said the prayers, and left. Priests oversaw everything, of course. The 'offerings' went to them. Some temples had dozens of priests and other staff, a Temple Cult. Size mattered. It was assumed that the largest temples with the most priests must be the most successful in communicating with their god/gods. (Sound familiar?)

Synagogues could hardly have been more different. There were no priests, only local, family people who had earned their places of respect and authority. Monetary offerings were accepted but went mainly to the poor. Judaism was based on trying to discover and follow the Will of the Loving God of Creation. People there talked, laughed, shared, ate, and debated. They were trying to get the most out of life, assuming that growing in love was most important. Gentiles were respected and welcomed to be among them, but there was no attempt to proselytize. All of humanity were understood as children of God. They didn't know of any Hell, for anyone.

This short time period, before the Jewish Revolt in 65 AD, was truly a Golden Age in Judaism. There were about ten million Jews in the Eastern Mediterranean. The Synagogue was often the second largest building in the city, only smaller than the Roman Coliseum. Because of the afore mentioned, many synagogues often had more Gentiles in attendance than Jews. It was the only place of reason and community for those who sought to grow, spiritually. These Gentiles were obviously those that Paul would approach with his 'Good News'.

In the years 40 to 65 AD, Saul (Paul, to the Gentiles) traveled from city to city in the eastern Mediterranean.

He preached to these Synagogue-worshipping Gentiles how the Way of Jesus was the Way of God, and organized them into communities of faith, following the Way of Jesus, adapting their own customs.

These groups soon became known as The People-of-the-Way.

It is essential for us to remember that every follower of Jesus, at this time, Jew and Gentile, assumed that the Risen Jesus/Christ/Messiah/Son of God, would return in the flesh, within their lifetimes, to end and restart creation. All of Paul's advice is given with this short-term assumption.

The People of the Way and Their Gospels

The Fall of Jerusalem in A.D. 70 shattered that understanding. The whole of the original community of followers must have died within its ancient walls because they are not heard from again. Paul was killed (probably) in Rome a few years before, at the outbreak of the Jewish Rebellion. Everyone had grossly misunderstood. All that was left of the Jesus Movement were the Gentile, Greek-thinking/believing communities that Paul and others had founded, then called The People-of-the-Way.

Few of these, however, were deterred. But it *was* going to be a 'longer haul' than they had thought. They had more time to wait and prepare for the Coming Messiah. How could they best use it? Tactics would have to change. Firstly, they'd better start writing things down. What we call the *Gospels* are the results of this need. Four writings were penned over the next thirty years, each written so people like them might hear, understand that God was in Jesus Christ, believe, and follow.

One of the hardest things for us to accept is that the Gospels were not written to answer *our* questions of history. As with all aspects of life, in our culture, we first want to know *what happened*: we automatically read the Gospels as if they're newspapers. Not so! History is there, all right, but the telling of it was/is *not* a priority. As you might have been noticed in the first of this writing, from the opening of the *Gospel of Luke,* the priority was to lead *those* people to faithfulness. It was to answer *their* questions, not *ours*. To them, 'History' as we think of it, was not of primary importance. In fact, as they understood it, 'history' would soon disappear with the Second Coming of Christ! The only things of history that were of importance to them were the sayings of Jesus and the barest outline of his last few days. These could not be overlooked.

So, some historical facts, stories and imagination were *all* used in the gospel narratives, all used to convey the good news of Eternal Salvation. The only thing that counted was the *fact* that the God of Creation was to be found in and through Jesus, their new Christ. The incidents of mere history were clearly secondary. If we truly want to understand what the Gospels have to say to us, we'd be wise to try to hear through the ears and minds of those first writers and readers.

Firstly and foremost, their truth had to be shared. They had found new life and meaning in the teachings of Jesus of Nazareth, the Christ, their Messiah, and Son of God. They knew that in believing and following him, they were part of the New People of God, that *they* had been Chosen to replace the Jews as God's Own. Nothing else mattered. The one and overriding purpose of the Gospels was to convey this reality.

In sharing this truth, there were several historical and immediate challenges. All knew the basic story of Jesus of Nazareth, that he was a rebellious Jew from Galilee (the center of all Jewish revolts), had led a movement that had confronted the rulers, and that he had been killed for crimes against Rome.

The first challenge for the Gospel writers was to tell the story so that Rome got 'off the hook' and wouldn't, in turn, try to kill them. Hadn't 'Rome' killed Paul, assuming a follower of Jesus would be a threat? It would have been an automatic assumption that to follow someone who had been killed by Rome, getting even (killing off some Romans) would be part of the initiation. The gospel writers knew this must *not* happen, for the Way of the new Christ was *non-violent*.

They were not writing in essay form, remember. They didn't explain using logic and reasons, as we would, but told their Truths in *story* form. *How* best to convey this truth was the challenge.

Recent history helped with this problem. The Jews had revolted against Rome and had lost. A commonly held assumption of that age was that the god's or God, *always* got their/His/Her way. From the Gentile's perspective, the God of Jesus/Christ/Messiah/Son of God, *must* have left the Jews, adopting the new believers as the new People of God. Why this assumption? Because the *Jews* had lost, while *they*, the Gentiles believers, were still alive and well. As further proof, by the time the Gospels were written, the Gentile followers of Jesus were already becoming suspect in their local synagogues, for they were increasingly equating Jesus Christ with God. They had found God through the teachings and person of Jesus, their Christ. Very soon the two blurred into one. This was in total opposition to the Jewish assumption that *God is One*. To the Jews, the Gentiles were tearing God into pieces: they were soon not welcomed.

Put these two facts together and the answer to the story-problem became obvious: Blame Jesus' death on the Jews and view Jesus' death as the ultimate sacrifice, not a scandal. (The Greeks could not imagine a religion *not* based upon Sacrifice.) Jews were a defeated and dispersed people anyway. From the perspective of the Gospel writers, it was a no-brainer. The scenario met all their needs. With the blame-switch storyline, new followers would understand how to act and what to believe, going forward in confidence and faithfulness.

With this common understanding, every Gospel, each in its own way, tells of how Jesus is the culmination, fulfilment, and termination of Judaism, what God really had in mind from the start of creation. Each writing assumes this stance. In the Gospel of John, for example, this is done by having *all* enemies of Jesus simply called, *The Jews*. He has no Roman enemies.

Setting the tone for the whole body of work is *Matthew*, by far the most antisemitic of the writings. It begins with a lengthy and contrived genealogy (differing from the one in *Luke*), showing the reader that Jesus is the culmination of the totality of Judaism. The first story tells of God having his Son born in the expected place (Bethlehem) and even has signs in the night sky, declaring the event to the whole world. Do any Jews have their eyes and hearts open enough to witness it? No. It takes three foreign Gentile astrologers to see the obvious. They go to Jerusalem and inquire. Only after they 'wake up' the officials, are the Jews aware of the Holy event. When the 'Wise Men' don't report back, King Herod-of-the-Jews does his best to kill the Holy Child. But his parents have escaped to Egypt after being warned by God of the danger from the Jewish throne.

It would be difficult to set the stage of Greek scriptures with a story more condemning to Jews. Through it, the readers were/are told that Jews are ignorant of God's Will, lazy, and want to kill Jesus from the first. Only Gentiles were *and are* on his side. (To hide this obvious message, we dress up children as 'Wise Men', and ignore the story.)

The whole of *Matthew* is written in five parts, clearly modeling its structure on the Jewish scriptures, symbolically replacing the Jewish Pentateuch. Jesus *must* go to Egypt to be able to return as the New Moses, giving his Sermon-on-the-Mount to replace Moses' reading when he came down from Mt. Sinai. Throughout *Matthew* are numerous places where the readers are told "these things came to pass so that the words" of certain scripture "might be fulfilled." This terminology enforces the understanding that the Jewish scripture, and Jews, are no longer needed. All has been replaced and made new in Christ.

To make sure the readers got the picture, in the trial scene at the grand-finale, 'bookending' the gospel, Pontius Pilate, one of the most notoriously cruel and able of Caesar's 'hatchet men', is portrayed as a weak and helpless Roman Governor, not being responsible in the least for Jesus' death. He publicly washes his hands of the whole affair, giving in to those dastardly Jews who, "*all, to the last man, demanded, 'Crucify him! Let his death be upon us and our children!*" (Mt. 27:26)

Is it a surprise that within a few centuries and there-after, Christians might come out of their Good Friday services to loot nearby Jewish shops and homes? To help us see the impossibility of this story being historical, let's transfer the scenario to occupied France under the Nazis.

The morning after a major insurrection by the French Resistance, the local Parisians, with no urging, bring their captured leader to the head of the German Gestapo, urging him to sentence their beloved former leader to death. The German not only doesn't recognize the rebel but finds no fault with him or what he has done. But, being frightened and intimidated by the ferociousness of the local French, he reluctantly does their bidding and sentences him to be shot, even when his wife tells him that the poor resistance leader had done no wrong.

Because the counterpart of this ludicrous scene is in the Bible, it has largely gone publicly unquestioned for nearly two millennia.

In the passion narratives, between the four Gospels, we have Jesus, somehow, in those few hours between when he was arrested, (around midnight?) and his 'trial' (9:00 AM.), taken to every possible official, Roman and Jewish. Who did the capturing of Jesus and 'escorted' him to the various officials and groups? Even though, barely half a day before, Jesus had publicly been welcomed as King, the number one crime against Rome, the gospels have no Romans involved. The readers are told that only Jews, from armed commoners to representatives of the Sanhedrin, High Priest and Temple Guards, took part. Historically, this is laughable. Remember that the Temple Guards, mainly ceremonial in duty, hadn't stopped Jesus-and-Friends from closing down the Temple, earlier that same day?

The Sanhedrin was the supreme council and highest Court of Justice in Jerusalem and in all of Judaism. The 71-member group was dominated by the priestly aristocracy and Sadducees but had representatives of most of the population, including lay members and representatives from the Scribes and Pharisees.

To further blame all Jews equally, we are told that the *whole* Sanhedrin was somehow brought together (at 2:00 AM?). (That governing body was forbidden to meet after sundown.) A consensus finds Jesus guilty, insisting that he be sent on to Pilate for execution. (In reality, the Sanhedrin *had* the authority to act. Had he been guilty of blasphemy, he could have been sentenced to death by stoning.) Let's unpack this pivotal but impossible scene, viewing it from history *and* from the eyes of Greek believers who were reading it some two generations later.

Since their conversions, the Greek followers had gleaned all the superlative titles from Jewish tradition, believing that they all *must* refer to Jesus of Nazareth.

They had come to know and believe him to be God Incarnate, so all those references and titles were *also* understood as divine, regardless of their original meanings. Although none of them, Messiah, Son of David, Son of God, had been divine titles to the original Jewish users, all these were synonymous to the Gentiles in their divine reference to Jesus, their Christ.

If there had been an interrogation of Jesus of Nazareth before the Sanhedrin, his claiming to be a messiah would have been foolish, for a messiah was a conqueror, not someone in chains. In no way, however, would it have been blasphemous. Others, before and after, would do so. Claiming to be God would have been blasphemous, but Jesus didn't do that. In fact, what the gospels have him saying is plausible. He had never said he desired to be a messiah. In fact, he had denied it at every opportunity. What the scene *does* truthfully tell the gospel readers is that the Jews didn't welcome Jesus as God-on-earth. That was indeed a fact. Jews could not imagine such a thing. A person might be *godly*, but that didn't imply their divinity.

The Greeks understood quite differently. Their old gods came to earth quite often. This scene, written for Greeks, reflects their realities. As used in the Greek Gospels, *Messiah* is the divine and eternal Son of

God, not a righteous King of the Jews. Although the story told did *not* happen, it *did* tell a *Truth* to the first readers. The Jews in Jesus' time had not believed he was what the Greeks later came to believe. Again, the writer of Matthew is telling this truth in story form. And it worked.

Squeezed into those few hours by the Gospel writers, is also a formal hearing before the High Priest, who finds him guilty. (There is no doubt the High Priest would indeed have loved to see him killed, for hadn't Jesus closed down his Temple and called him a thief?) There is another farcical scene where Jesus is taken before King Herod Antipas who just happens to be in town. Of course, Herod (acting as a Roman official now), finds no fault with him, even though, in fact Herod, shortly before, had killed Jesus' mentor, John the Baptist, for much less.

The Gospel writers leave no stone unturned to tell us that Jews are totally responsible for Jesus' death and all possible Roman authorities were innocent, only participating in the unjust affair because of the pressure put upon them by the hate-filled, unfaithful Jews. In the Coptic Church, Pontius Pilate was even declared a Saint!

In the whole of all four Gospels there is not one 'bad' Roman. Not one soldier or official takes advantage of their position. Not one rape, death, or abuse is hinted of, apart from John the Baptist (Luke 3: 12-14). No mention of Caesar or the hated Romans and their occupation. Also, the word 'Jew' is never used in the positive. Jesus' followers, though obviously Jews, are never mentioned as such. It's as though they have acquired a new heritage. *Jew* is usually a negative connotation.

If we were to pick up a book written in any time of military occupation, be it Ireland in the early 1900s, or Norway in 1944, and there was no mention of oppression by the Germans or English occupiers, wouldn't we wonder why? If the terms *Norwegians* or *Irish* were never used in a positive way, wouldn't we be surprised? And question?

For 1800 years, Sunday after Sunday, word by word, inferences time and again, the story line has molded the minds and assumptions of the listeners. The Gospel writers were more successful than they could have imagined. Not only did their work succeed in their lifetime, but it has also molded Christians into the nemesis of Judaism ever since. Not that all who persecute Jews today are Christians. The lie has become such a part of our Western culture that it crops up unexpectedly, within most conspiracy theories and unrelated hatred. It is hard to find a current world-plot conspiracy that doesn't include, in one way or another, Jews trying to dominate the world.

How dismayed the gospel writers would be if they could see that the results of their successful efforts would lead to such tragedy. How could they know that future Gentiles would so betray Jesus' Way of non-violence?

But the source is never acknowledged. Many churches have apologized for any part in the holocaust, but none has acknowledged the accepted but hidden fire that kindled the tragedy. The Second Vatican Council in 1963 exonerated Jews as the killers of Jesus but left it at that. In all churches there are numerous and beautiful prayers for peace and justice. Never is there a hint that words of scripture read from the pulpits often have the exact opposite effect.

A personal example: One of my favorite Christmas songs, one I and my family have treasured since my childhood, is *Sweet Little Jesus Boy*, a black slave spiritual some two-hundred years old. The first line goes, *Sweet little Jesus, boy, they made you be born in a manger.* I have sung this song over a hundred times. It wasn't until this week that I really looked at the words in that first line. Who are the THEY that were so evil that

THEY made the Son of God to be born in a barn? Jews, of course! I'm going to have to change those words or continue to be complicit in the ongoing tragedy of authorized and systemic anti-Semitism.

Sadly, few, if any, churchgoers will take this seriously. There's just too much at stake as far as their self-identity and assumed religiosity are concerned. Few pastors will risk their jobs to talk about it: the number one rule of any pastorate is to not 'rock the boat' and verbalizing this question would surely disturb. Since the 300's AD when Christianity was imposed on the Roman Empire by Constantine the Great, the Laity, by definition, were *not* to question the newly established priests. Their role was/is to listen to those who are licensed, trained and ordained to speak the traditional truth. So, from the pulpit or pew, in all Christian traditions, there's no reason to expect any change but the doubling down on the norm.

The End of the People-of-the-Way

One of the main tenants of the followers of Jesus had been the assumption of Non-Violence. As we have seen, in the Gospels, blame for Jesus' death had been shifted to the Jews for just that reason, to keep people from seeking violent revenge upon the Romans. In the short term, the ploy seemed to work. But not for long. History shows us the vitriol within the gospels was activated even before Emperor Constantine gave his new Christianity, power. Constantine had adopted and formed Christianity because, among other things, he was having a hard time finding soldiers for his army. Followers of Jesus wouldn't fight. After the Council of Nicaea in 325 AD, the new rules allowed 'Christian' soldiers to fight for God and Empire. In this one stroke, the People of the Way, the Jesus Movement, ceased to exist.

With the assumption of non-violence shattered, sectarian violence soon became a fact, with Christians being 'blessed' in not only killing Jews and other

Pagans, but other Christians who didn't agree with them. Think of *the Jesus Wars* in the 400s AD. (There's a great book by Philip Jenkins with this title) when it became acceptable for Christians to kill each other if they disagreed over doctrine. Think of the numerous religious wars, or the even more common wars between 'good Christians', such as in the Ukraine, where, predictably, both sides *know* that God is on their side. Try to find, today, a major Christian group that is adamantly against violence. Only smaller groups such as the Quakers, Amish and Mennonites are trying to be faithful to this most basic of Jesus' teachings.

The approved antisemitism in the Gospels has been foundational to this Christian habit that has been so detrimental to us all. In retrospect, the gospel-writers failed miserably. Instead of curbing violence, they sowed its seeds to the wind and provided fertile ground. Unknowingly, they traded short-term gain for untold pain upon Judaism and also implanted a cancerous blight within the eventual Christian religion.

What now?

I find myself feeling very close to the writers of the Gospels. I, too, am wondering just how to write my 'account' that will lead others to faithfulness and hope. I've done my best to present my 'case' of things that have led to now, but that's only preamble to what is important. If the future isn't changed, it has all been wasted. And how can I, or We, attempt to affect an illness that is so deep within the very genes of our culture, and whose seed lies, still festering, within the world's largest religion, in its most sacrosanct scriptures?

The first source of hope must lie within that very religion itself. For it is based upon love. We must share the assumption that "*the truth will set us free.*" I am no naïve five-year-old, assuring you that 'everything will be all right', nor do I believe that 'in the end, God's Will *will* be done.

ERIC HOTZ © 2017

37

Remember that I'm a follower of Jesus of Nazareth, and things didn't go so well for him.

But I also know that God's Spirit, however you might understand that power, is alive and well, even if mostly hidden or unrecognized. The fact that most 'mainline' churches are in decline tells us that something quite basic is missing in them. Perhaps the airing of this reality will be a way for them to rediscover the wonder of their scriptures and the love and life that can come from them. If the scriptures involved are brought to light and debated, what harm can it do?

So, people within churches, what you can do is just that: dare to talk about this. Share this book. Know that your fellow parishioners won't jump for joy, but they will, I promise you, listen and react. And any reaction is a sign of life. That just might be what your church needs.

What about out-of-churchers? You too, of course, have news to share with those around you. But one more avenue of action comes to mind. The very sad but obvious fact is, according to our modern definition, some passages of the gospels, particularly *Matthew* and *John*, can easily be classified as *hate literature*. In our culture, nothing gets the attention of news outlets and viewers more than scandalous legal action.

Are there a few lawyers that would take on the case of charging the publishers and distributors of Bibles with contributing to or supporting hate crimes? Or any other such actions? I know that these would be doomed to failure, legally, but it *would* bring the facts to light, educating as well as disturbing. Think of the Scopes Trial a century ago that was between a school board and a science teacher, deciding if the Theory of Evolution could be taught in the local school. The legal outcome supported the Creationists, but the truth was aired to the whole world. The trial was instrumental in winning, on many levels, the war (that is, sadly, still being fought.) Biblical scripture was released from a tradition of smallness and fear. This could happen again. It is certainly needed.

But I certainly won't be leading this charge. What I *can* do is promise to set all earnings from this book aside, available for any such legal purposes. I urge others to do the same. Are there any (or one) who would set up such a fund to which we can contribute? I will do my utmost to support any such efforts, but my time, knowledge and energy is limited.

It's time now for some good news, a story that is current and gives us hope. It comes straight out of the April 2023 issue of *Sojourners* magazine. I encourage you to subscribe.

In 1633, the Bavarian village of Oberammergau experienced a miracle. The villagers promised God they would stage an annual reenactment of the Passion of Christ if they were spared from the plague. They were. Nearly 400 years later, people continue to come from around the world to see the performances. But there's a problem. Oberammergau's Passion Play is one of the most antisemitic artworks in history. Adolph Hitler attended twice, in 1930 and again in 1934, for inspiration and ideas. It's straight out of *John* and *Matthew*.

The good news is that, finally, things have changed. Recently, rather than continuing to ignore and continue with the hate-filled tradition, the director worked with the American Jewish Committee to rid the play of anti-Jewish tropes. The 2022 production tried to tell a more complete and historically accurate Easter story. "The Jews" now include Jesus and his followers. Jesus lifts a copy of the Torah to pray the Sh'ma Yisrael. Hebrew prayers were recited at the Last Supper. Significantly, the updated version calls Christians to repent for how we've failed in our foundational sibling relationship. (The above is mostly quoted from *Sojourners*.)

How wonderful it is to see that people can learn, and change. If this most traditional and venerated event/pilgrimage site can correct itself, there's real hope.

Closing

As clergy and friend, I have had the honor to be at the bedside of many who were approaching death. The saddest words shared to me were ones of regret of having not done what they knew was most important. I have often vowed that I would have no such words to share. I can easily say that in the writing and sharing of this, much of that possibility is relieved.

I have hope because I know people's minds can be changed. We *can* learn. Even a few can make a difference. All great movements start with a few people around a table, or on-line. I know also that the world is in terrible shape. We are killing each other and the world and usually remain blind and ignore our reality. Our challenges seem so enormous that we've mainly lost hope. But this one focus might lead to bigger things. If just a few of us can try to excise this blight and provide hope for a better future of even a few, the effort will be worthwhile.

And, thankfully, success breeds success. Hope is contagious. It brings joy, and that is the enemy of fear. Even a small conspiracy against fear, ignorance and violence might be recognized and have a positive effect on our most needy world. I most humbly invite any and all of you to see the immediacy and urgency of this project. Any action you *Do* will influence others and will change the future for Jews and for Christians

Personal footnote

I apologize deeply for not writing this, years sooner. I was raised within Christianity, the youngest elder in the United Church of Canada at one time, have led youth groups and choirs, gained a M. Div. and was ordained clergy for twenty years. I've known this stuff for a long time but have just now put it all together. If there are negative personal reactions to this, I've little to lose. I have already burned most bridges with churches. The writing of this is just one more. But proclaim this truth, I must. We are all called to share the 'Words of God' that come to us. That is what I am doing. Thank you for lending me your ears. I sincerely welcome any feedback, especially, your support. I can make no difference alone. The road ahead will be rocky.

Shalom,

Anthony.

anthonygifford42@gmail.com

Anthonygiffford.ca

Addendum

Dear 'Theophilus', there's a very good chance that much of the basic scholarship and facts that I've shared, is news to you. What were your reactions? Did you think I was inventing things, or that I've discovered them on my own? Did you doubt them with the assumption that I was somehow going to personally benefit from the 'inventions'? Did they bring to mind numerous times that you've heard others preach an opposite meaning? What were/are your feelings? Anger? Dismay? Excitement? Joy? Threat? Don't feel alone. I've been there.

I was as 'well-churched' as most. But a questioner. I had graduated in Education with minors in mathematics, music and physics. Even before graduation, Dad and I bought a cattle ranch in central British Columbia. My wife and I moved in, ran the ranch and taught in a nearby school. Over the next twelve years my spiritual journey grew to the point that when Dad suddenly died, and I was unable to raise finances for the purchase of his half, we sold the ranch. The sale left enough funds that allowed me to take a few years off. So, I enrolled in a seminary, not to become clergy, but to learn and to have my questions answered.

Even today, I still remember when, after just two weeks, I was filled with two conflicting emotions: anger and elation. On one hand, I was joyous. The Bible made sense! It was challenging and real! On the other, was anger. Why had these things not been told me before? Why had church and Bible Study been so boring? Why had well accepted biblical scholarship not been shared from the pulpit? Why was I ignorant of this after thirty-three years of sitting in a pew? As I recall, this awareness happened as we were studying *Matthew*, the gospel which is so pivotal in this writing.

I was able to deal with the contradictions and emotions, and stayed within Christianity (until recently). But many who are confronted with the contradictions between church teachings and biblical scholarship, aren't able to reconcile the two. Numerous young Christians 'lose their faith' when, in *Gospels 101*, at most accredited universities (*not* bible colleges) they find that they've been lied to and deceived by their churches. The consequence is, that very often, they come to reject the very idea of 'religion'. The baby is truly tossed out with the bath water.

Christianity is now divided into two broad groups. One denies Biblical questioning and scholarship, labeling it demonic. The other claims to accept it, in principle, but basically ignores it and its implications, seeming to be unable to replace *Belief* in biblical fundamentalism with *discipleship*. The simplicity of the first group maintains its attractiveness to many. The second, the traditional *Mainline Churches*, are predictably dying, for they have little to offer.

Regardless of our origins, few of us have been exposed to ideas and biblical knowledge that has been standard fare for at least a century. All churches, no matter their origins, for their own reasons, have kept this to themselves. It is expected that any who read this booklet will be challenged, one way or another. Again, thanks for sticking with me, accepting the challenge, in hopes that better and more Holy days are ahead. Don't hesitate to get in touch.

Anthony,

In hopes that the Gospels, as intended, may result only in Love.

Printed in Dunstable, United Kingdom